CW00457571

KINGSTON AND HOUNSLOW LOOPS

including the Shepperton Branch

Vic Mitchell and Keith Smith

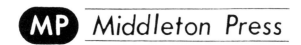

MP Middleton Press

Cover picture: Two 3-coach sets pass Hounslow goods shed and water tank, displaying the loop headcode. The dash over the O indicated that Richmond was visited before Hounslow.
(Lens of Sutton)

First published October 1990
Reprinted November 1997

ISBN 0 906520 83 5

© *Middleton Press, 1990*

Design - Deborah Goodridge

Published by
        Middleton Press
        Easebourne Lane
        Midhurst, West Sussex
        GU29 9AZ
Tel: 01730 813169
Fax: 01730 812601

Printed & bound by Biddles Ltd,
        Guildford and Kings Lynn

CONTENTS

Section 1   Kingston Loop   1 - 37
Section 2   Shepperton Branch   38 - 70
Section 3   Hounslow Loop   71 - 120

71	Barnes		
73	Barnes Bridge	83	Kew Bridge, East of
78	Chiswick	92	Kew Bridge, West of
39	Fulwell	8	Kingston
38	Fulwell Junction	1	Malden
43	Hampton	3	Norbiton
49	Hampton Waterworks	62	Shepperton
16	Hampton Wick	32	Strawberry Hill
106	Hounslow	26	Strawberry Hill Depot
119	Hounslow Junction	54	Sunbury
102	Isleworth	98	Syon Lane
51	Kempton Park	21	Teddington
85	Kew Bridge	59	Upper Halliford

ACKNOWLEDGEMENTS

In addition to many of the photographers credited in the captions, we have received help from R.M.Casserley, D.Clayton, C.R.L.Coles, M.J.Furnell, J.B.Horne, J.R.W.Kirkby, J.Morel, D.Pede, R.Randell, A.Regan, R.C.Riley, E.Staff and N.Stanyon.   Tickets have been provided by G.Croughton and N.Langridge. We are very grateful to all these contributors, and to our wives for their endless assistance.

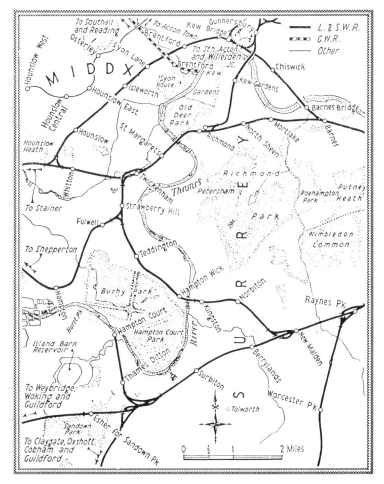

Map of the Kingston and Hounslow Loops, showing pre-grouping ownership and one subsequent station - Syon Lane. (Railway Magazine)

HISTORICAL BACKGROUND

The first lines south-westwards from London were to Woking Common (opened 21st May 1838) and to Richmond (opened 27th July 1846). The latter was extended to Staines and Datchet on 27th August 1848. The Windsor & South Western Railway opened its line from Barnes to Smallberry Green (Isleworth) on 22nd August 1849 and extended it to Hounslow and Feltham Junction on 1st February 1850. All these routes had come under the control of the London and South Western Railway by July 1850.

A line between Old Kew Junction and Willesden Junction was opened on 1st August 1853 by the North & South Western Junction Railway, which was owned jointly by the London & North Western, North London and Midland Railways. The NLR operated the passenger trains, while the LSWR provided the goods services.

The first Kingston station was on the London & Southampton Railway and was renamed Surbiton after the town received a branch from Twickenham on 1st July 1863. (In 1834, Kingston Corporation had been the main objector to the main line being routed closer to the town). The Shepperton branch, or Thames Valley Line, opened on 1st November 1864, as a single line, being doubled in 1878 when Kempton Park race traffic started. Access to the branch was from the Twickenham direction only. The Malden-Kingston section came into use on 1st January 1869, at last giving the residents of Kingston a direct route to London.

The spur between the Hounslow and Twickenham lines was opened on 1st January 1883, enabling trains to operate a circular route from Waterloo. The spur south of Strawberry Hill Depot first carried passenger trains between Kingston and Shepperton on 1st June 1901. Electrification of the Kingston Loop and Shepperton branch took place on 30th January 1916 and the Hounslow Loop followed on 12th March of the same year.

The transition to Southern Railway in 1923 and to British Railways in 1948 had little effect on passenger services but freight facilities were largely withdrawn in the mid-1960s.

GEOGRAPHICAL SETTING

The routes are all within the lower Thames Valley and cross the Gravels of the river terraces, although Brickearth is present in the Kingston area.

Between Fulwell and Hampton the Shepperton branch is in a cutting enabling it to pass under the Longford River, which was constructed in the 17th century to convey fresh water to Hampton Court Palace from the River Colne.

All maps are to the scale of 25" to 1 mile, unless otherwise specified.

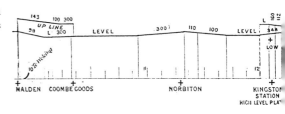

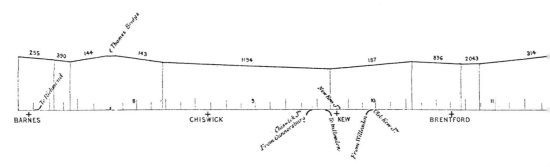

PASSENGER SERVICES

The Sunday frequency is shown in brackets.

Kingston Loop

The first timetables showed about 14 trains on weekdays between London and Kingston via Twickenham, 5 from Waterloo and 9 from Fenchurch Street via Barnes Bridge and the North London Railway. This circuitous service ceased in 1869, after which date NLR trains terminated at Richmond, using the new line through Kew Gardens.

From 1866 Kingston residents could travel to the City via Richmond, Clapham Junction and Loughborough Junction to Ludgate Hill. In 1869 these through trains were replaced by a new service of 11 (4) trains being provided, all terminating at Ludgate Hill. At this time a service of 23 (13) trains to Waterloo via Twickenham was introduced. By 1890, the Waterloo service comprised 27 (16) on this route and 26 (8) via Wimbledon. By 1906 the corresponding figures were 31 (15) and 38 (20), a dramatic increase reflecting the way in which the railway developed the area for residential purposes.

Electrification in 1916 brought four trains an hour to the Kingston loop daily, in addition to the Shepperton service. This high frequency was maintained until the advent of World War II, when some reduction was instituted. In the summers of 1930 to 1937, there was a Sundays only train between Kingston and Ramsgate, which broke the clockwork regularity of the "Southern Electric". Until WWII, there were three journeys each way during the night which were steam hauled, as the current was switched off to avoid the need to man the rotary converter sub-stations at night.

The "Kingston Roundabout" survived, albeit at reduced frequency, until May 1985. Subsequently most trains from Waterloo via Twickenham have terminated at Kingston.

June 1869

Shepperton Branch

The initial service was one of seven trains each way on weekdays. By 1869 there were 11 (5), increasing to 20 (6) in 1890 and 26 (9) by 1906, another example of successful stimulation of residential development by the LSWR. From 1901 until electrification in 1916, all but one weekday train ran via Twickenham but thereafter the reverse has applied with only a few peak and some Sunday services not being run via Kingston. Two trains per hour daily was the initial basic electric service and this has remained unchanged, apart from Sunday reductions and wartime curtailments. There have been periods of economy when the branch service has terminated at Kingston but they have not been long lived.

Hounslow Loop

The train service frequency from Waterloo to Hounslow via Kew Bridge over the sample years was as follows: 1869 - 19 (12), 1890 - 29 (13) and 1906 - 34 (13). The number of trains continuing to Feltham or beyond were 10, 15 and 17, respectively.

From 1883, this line saw a service from Gunnersbury to Twickenham via Kew Bridge and Hounslow, providing the only trains over the Hounslow Junction to Whitton Junction curve. In the years before WWI this service was worked by steam rail motors; it ran for the last time on 21 February 1915.

Electrification brought a basic half-hourly weekday roundabout service, hourly on Sundays. This was increased to half-hourly in the summers after WWI, to cater for summer riverside traffic.

Little changed until May 1987, when the roundabout service largely ceased, trains terminating alternately at Weybridge and Woking. In May 1989, Guildford became the terminal point for all Hounslow line trains, except a few in the peak hours, and a 30 minute interval service has been largely maintained.

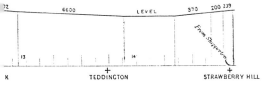

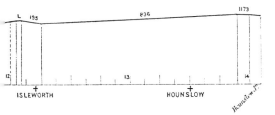

1. KINGSTON LOOP
NEW MALDEN

1. The main line to the West of England is on the left, as class M7 0-4-4T no. 30248 climbs up the connection from the Kingston Loop on 10th July 1954. The empty coaches had left Strawberry Hill at 8.39am and would be later used for the 9.30 Waterloo to Bournemouth, one of the many extra holiday trains then run on summer Saturdays. They are viewed from the island platform at Malden - the suffix "New" was not added until September 1957. (J.H.Aston)

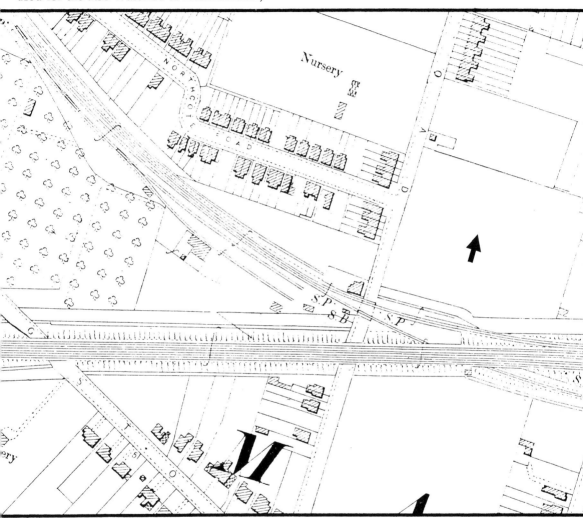

2. The 12.55 from Shepperton is seen from the main line embankment on 11th December 1978. An industrial building occupies the site of the goods yard, which closed on 3rd September 1964. Full lifting barriers were installed in November 1974, when the box became a gate box. It closed in January 1979, when CCTV was installed, supervised from Feltham. A second track passed under the main line until about 1884. (J.Scrace)

Malden station is beyond the right margin of this 1897 map and since it was built on an embankment, the goods yard (centre) was remote from it. An additional coal siding and a goods shed were provided later and, further east, a private siding was laid for Twisteel Ltd.

Photographs of New Malden station and maps of the junction appear in our *Waterloo to Woking* album.

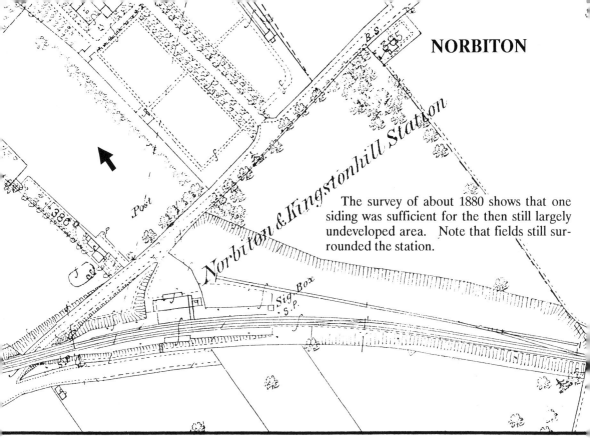

NORBITON

The survey of about 1880 shows that one siding was sufficient for the then still largely undeveloped area. Note that fields still surrounded the station.

3. The station opened with the line on 1st January 1869 and was gracious and spacious, in keeping with many of the new houses in the locality. Earlier Surbiton had developed owing to the proximity of a new station - now it was the turn of the area east of Kingston. (Lens of Sutton)

4. Extensive weather protection for London bound passengers was provided as an inducement to potential house purchasers/ passengers. They could find scant provision on other suburban stations, notably those on the South Eastern Railway. (Lens of Sutton)

The 1913 edition indicates only a few empty building plots and an expansion of goods facilities, although no shed or crane were provided. A 300yd long down refuge siding is seen to curve under Gloucester Road bridge, on the right.

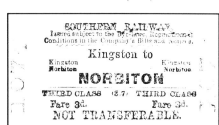

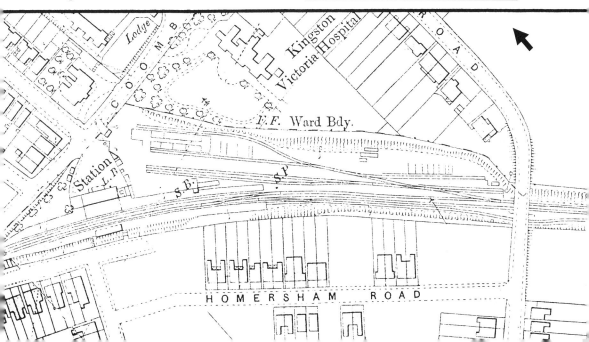

5. A train from Waterloo via Twickenham makes an unusual reversal at Norbiton on 10th May 1959, the inverted headcode indicating that unit no. 4306 is empty. P was the headcode for Waterloo to Kingston via Twickenham. For most of the 1950s, the heap of scrap metal on the left partly obscured a narrow gauge industrial locomotive of the Bagnall type. (J.H.Aston)

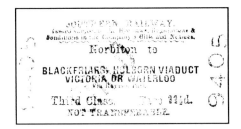

SOUTHERN RAILWAY.
Issued subject to the Bye-Laws, Regulations &
Conditions in the Company's Bills and Notices.

Norbiton to

BLACKFRIARS, HOLBORN VIADUCT
VICTORIA OR WATERLOO
Via Raynes Park

Third Class — Fare 11½d.
NOT TRANSFERABLE.

0837

SOUTHERN RAILWAY.
This Ticket is issued subject to the Bye-laws
Regulations & Conditions stated in the
Company's Time Tables Bills & Notices

NORBITON to
ISLEWORTH
Via Twickenham

Norbiton   Norbiton
Isleworth   Isleworth
3rd CLASS   3rd CLASS
Fare 10d   Fare 10d

0837

6. On the same day, 4SUB no. 4681 has just used the crossover owing to the closure of Elm Road level crossing, seen in picture no. 2. In 1990, the buildings on both sides remained standing, the canopy had been re-roofed but the glazed screen on the left was no longer present. (J.H.Aston)

7. Photographed in 1968, the lofty signal box remained in use until 27th July 1969. The goods yard behind it had closed on 3rd May 1965. Through trains are subject to a 50 mph speed limit here. (J.Scrace)

KINGSTON

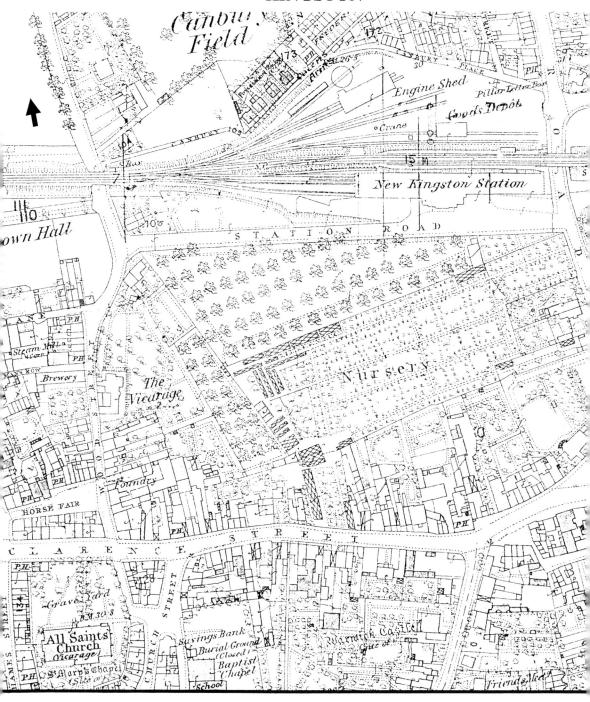

The 1880 edition marks the position of the engine shed, which in 1898 became the goods shed and was still standing in 1990. Note the orchard and nursery separating the town from the station.

8.   From 1863 until 1869, Kingston was a terminus for trains from the Teddington direction only. This later view shows the train shed which accommodated three terminal platforms.   The footway to the two high level through platforms is on the right. The tracks in the foreground carried trams from 1906 until 1931. (Lens of Sutton)

9. The roof covering the terminal platforms is on the right in this view towards Norbiton. The small signal box in the distance controlled access to the coal yard.   In the mid-1880s, the platforms had been rebuilt and a concourse provided at the low level. (Lens of Sutton)

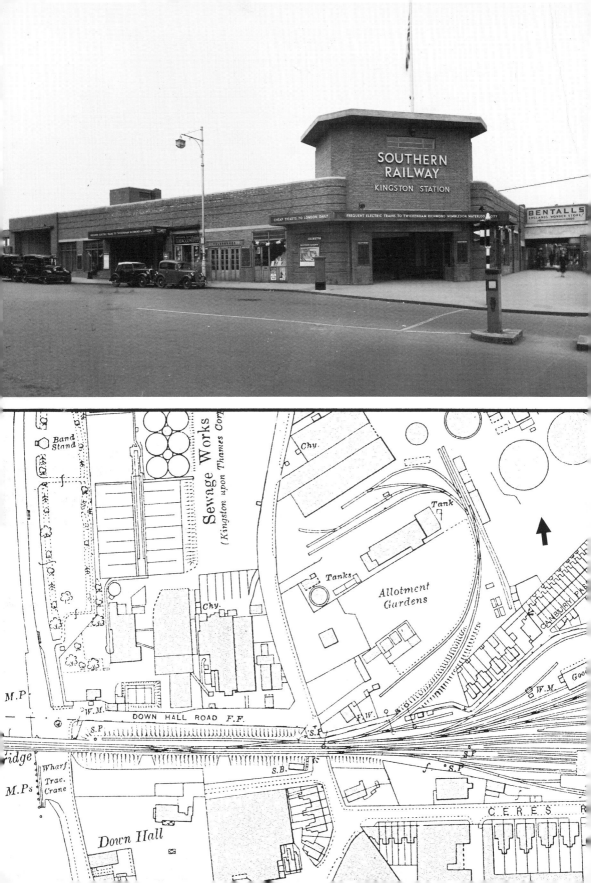

SOUTHERN RAILWAY

KINGSTON STATION

CHEAP TICKETS TO LONDON DAILY

FREQUENT ELECTRIC TRAINS TO TWICKENHAM RICHMOND WIMBLEDON WATERLOO CITY

BENTALLS
ENGLANDS WONDER STORE

Band Stand

Sewage Works
(Kingston upon Thames Corp.

Chy.

Tank

Tanks

Allotment Gardens

CANBURY PARK

Chy.

M.P

W.M.

DOWN HALL ROAD F.F.

S.P.

W.M.

Goo

ridge

S.P.

S.B.

S.P.

Wharf
Trac.
Crane

S.P.

M.Ps

CERES R

Down Hall

10. The station was completely rebuilt in 1934-35, when one bay platform was rebuilt at a higher level. Two subways were constructed, the one visible on the right being for public use. The total cost was £40,000. (N.Langridge coll.)

11. On 17th December 1960, a Christmas parcels special was composed of vans and old coaches. This traffic was often carried in electric stock, with the seat cushions reversed. The buildings on the right were occupied by meat wholesalers, no doubt supplied by rail in earlier years. (J.J.Smith)

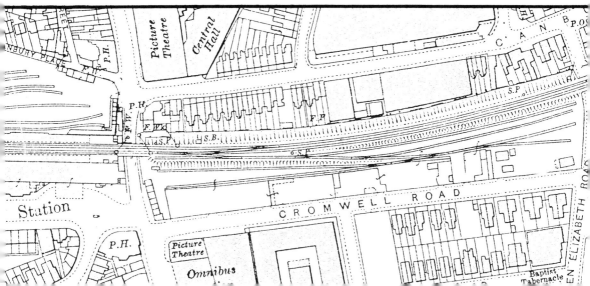

The 1932 survey reveals the extent of the goods yard improvements and the size of the supplementary coal yard, adjacent to Cromwell Road. Private sidings were provided for the Kingston Gas Co. and the Anglo-American Oil Depot. The gasworks siding was also extended later into the sewage works.

12. Driver Ralph Collins waits to leave the bay platform on 22nd April 1967 with a Waterloo via Twickenham service. After WWII, the site of the earlier bay platforms was used as a satellite bus station for routes 85, 131, 213 and 216. No. 264 and some London Country services also used it later. (R.E.Ruffell)

14. A telephoto view across the Thames from Kingston shows 4 EPB no. 5123 forming the 10.26 from Shepperton on 11th May 1983. Behind it is Hampton Wick station and in the distance are the gas holders of the former Hampton Court Gas Co. (C.Wilson)

13. Two newly delivered class 455 units work a down service on 11th May 1983. Between the wars, a siding terminated near the huts on the left to serve the Kingston Corporation Electricity Works, which was in Down Hall Road. In 1989, a new road bridge was built under the end of the down platforms to serve a circulatory system in which the station is in the centre. The former loco/goods shed is beyond the third coach. (C.Wilson)

0590

SOUTHERN RAILWAY.
This ticket is not transferable and is issued subject to the Company's Bye-laws, Regulations and Conditions in their Time Tables, Notices and Book of Regulations.

Kingston   to

Kingston   Kingston
Richmond or   Richmond or
St. Margaret's   St. Margaret's
RICHMOND or ST. MARGARET'S
THIRD CLASS (S.20)   THIRD CLASS
Fare 5d.   Fare 5d.

0590

15. On 25th March 1962, class O2 0-4-4T no. 30199 headed westwards with an REC railtour of South London lines. The train was composed of ex-LMS non-corridor coaches. The power station was built soon after WWII, but its coal requirements were water borne. (J.J.Smith)

SOUTHERN RAILWAY.

Kingston to

Kingston	Kingston
Richmond or	Richmond or
St. Margarets	St. Margarets

RICHMOND or
ST. MARGARETS

THIRD CLASS (S.22) THIRD CLASS
Fare 5½d   Fare 5½d

FOR CONDITIONS SEE BACK

7101   7103

HAMPTON WICK

16. Until 24th September 1916, this signal box stood on the down platform, at the far end of which the line drops at 1 in 102 towards Teddington. All structures were of timber, to reduce weight on the embankment. (Lens of Sutton)

17. Round headed windows and doors were notable features of the ground level buildings and numerous other LSWR stations built in the 1860s. Note the street rails of the railway's competitor, which passed close to all stations to Richmond. The bridge over the main road was the scene of a serious head on collision between a light engine and a train from Waterloo via Twickenham on 6 August 1888, in which three people were killed and fifteen injured. (Lens of Sutton)

18.   Cranes tower above Kingston during major rebuilding works in 1989, as a class 455 unit leaves for Shepperton. The station was rebuilt in 1969, using CLASP prefabricated units and concrete platform slabs. (J.Scrace)

19. The south elevation reveals BR architecture at its most featureless and the decoration at its most unimaginative (black and white). Thankfully, both have improved dramatically elsewhere in later years, but Hampton Wick has only received a repaint. (J.Scrace)

20.　A loop line service proceeds towards Teddington on 8th May 1970 and passes over Fairfax Road crossing.　Until 1961, the space on the right was crossed by a long siding to the gasworks. Dozing passengers could always tell their location by the smell pervading this district.　The signal box opened on 24th September 1916, when full gates replaced the agricultural type.　The box and crossing were both closed on 30th April 1973.　(J.Scrace)

The 1934 map shows five lines on the right. The lower three were used for the storage of steam-hauled coaches used only at peak holiday periods.　Earlier these sidings had served gravel pits which were later filled in with rubbish.　One siding was extended to the gasworks, over half a mile from Teddington station.　In 1947, the works received 40,000 tons of coal and large quantities of firebrick, and despatched by rail 19,000 tons of coke, 447,000 gallons of tar and substantial volumes of ammoniacal liquor.

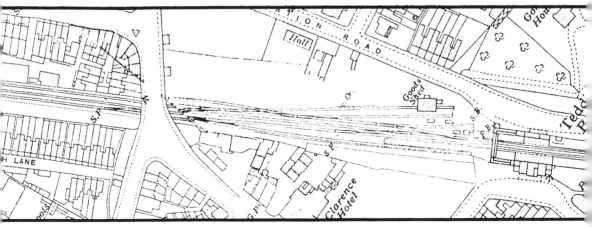

TEDDINGTON

21. This impressive building was erected on the down side and was of similar design to those built earlier at Chertsey and at Staines, although here the central portion projects, instead of being recessed. All three were still standing in 1990. (Lens of Sutton)

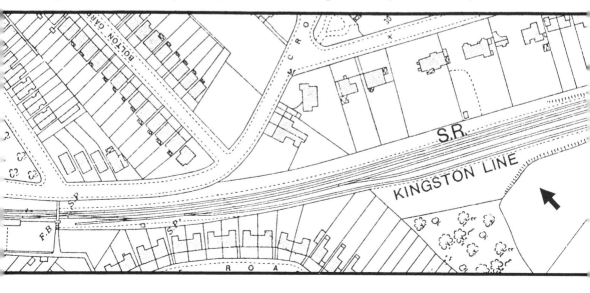

22. Two 3SUBs depart north in the late 1930s, the nearer one having been built in 1925. Two trailer coaches (ex-steam and fitted with jumper cables) were marshalled between these sets at peak periods until 1948. By this time, an additional coach had been inserted to form 4SUBs. (J.W.Sparrowe)

23. At the south end of the platforms, the line was crossed by a public footbridge, from which the previous photograph was taken. This 1956 view shows a shunting operation which delayed an up passenger train. Having shunted the goods yard, the locomotive had propelled its train through the platforms and was about to use the crossover prior to returning to Feltham Yard. The locomotive is no. 30567, one of the 0395 class 0-6-0s and built in 1883. (V.Mitchell)

⟶

25. Unit no. 5838 accelerates towards Strawberry Hill on 29th June 1985, passing the site of a single siding that once served a loading dock, then obscured by bushes. Commercial premises occupy the site of the goods yard, on the left. Before reaching Shacklegate Junction, the train would pass the site of Somerset Road level crossing, which was abolished on 14th June 1964. (C.Wilson)

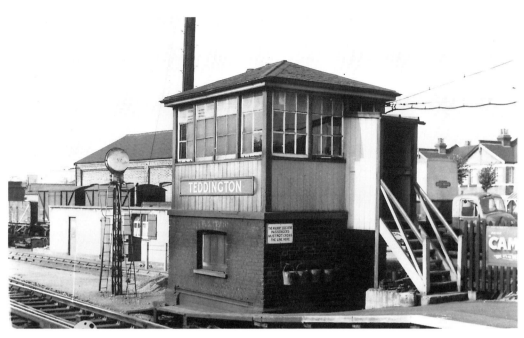

24. A Scammell mechanical horse and the goods shed are partly obscured by the signal box, which was closed on 3rd January 1966. The goods yard had a crane of 4 tons 11cwt capacity and was closed on 3rd May 1965. (D.Cullum coll.)

STRAWBERRY HILL DEPOT

26.   Built in 1897, the depot could house 30 locomotives, including those formerly shedded at Kingston and Twickenham. It was enlarged in 1906 to accommodate 50 engines and is seen in these three photographs in April 1923. No. 520 is one of the five class H16 4-6-2Ts built in the previous two years for heavy freight work. (H.C.Casserley)

27. The coal stage, water tank and water softening tower are included in this northward view, Strawberry Hill station footbridge being visible in the distance. Class T1 no. 77 was built in 1890 and scrapped in 1932. (H.C.Casserley)

28. Viewed from the water tank, Strawberry Hill signal box is in the distance and class M7 no. 377 stands in front of class T1 no. 77. The fan of sidings (on the left) led to the nine shed roads which were electrified in 1916, steam locomotives being transferred to the new shed at Feltham in 1923. (H.C.Casserley)

29. A closer view of the depot in 1970 shows the four berthing sidings outside the shed. In 1907 a new 50ft diameter turntable was installed on the area of waste land beyond the buffer stops. By 1938, there were eleven 8-coach trains allocated here. (R.E.Ruffell)

30. A panorama of the north end of the depot in 1972 includes the former steam repair shop, by then trackless. On the right, a main line 4CIG unit is visible. This class was not allocated to the depot but was berthed and cleaned during the day. Extreme right, the former coal dump sidings have latterly been used for the storage of redundant or damaged stock. (R.E.Ruffell)

31. The depot is viewed from the south from Shacklegate Lane bridge in August 1952. The line to Shepperton curves to the left, while the Twickenham route is on the right. Down trains on this route become up trains to Waterloo via Kingston at Shacklegate Junction and vice versa. The box closed on 10th November 1972. (D.Cullum)

SOUTHERN RLY.
Issued subject to the
Bye-laws, Regulations and
Conditions in the Company's
Bills and Notices.
Norbiton to
(8.10)
BLACKFRIARS,
HOLBORN VIAD'T
VICTORIA
or WATERLOO
Via Raynes Park
Third Cl. Fare 1/8
Not Transferable

SOUTHERN RLY.
Issued subject to the
Bye-laws, Regulations and
Conditions in the Company's
Bills and Notices.
Norbiton to
(8.9)
BLACKFRIARS,
HOLBORN VIAD'T
VICTORIA
or WATERLOO
Via Raynes Park
Third Cl. Fare 1/8
Not Transferable.

32. The station opened over ten years after the Kingston branch from Twickenham, on 1st December 1873. This northward view shows that the main buildings were, unusually, on the down side. (Lens of Sutton)

33. The signal box probably dates from the opening of the depot in 1897, its predecessor being on the opposite side of the track since the opening of the Shepperton branch in 1864. The box was originally named "Thames Valley Junction". (Lens of Sutton)

This 1934 map has the line to Shepperton top left; to Teddington lower left and to Twickenham lower right. Shacklegate Junction is lower left and Fulwell Junction is at the top of the triangle. Although marked as an engine shed, the building had been used for EMUs since 1923. The southern part of the triangle was opened to goods traffic on 1st July 1894 and to passengers on 1st June 1901.

War Meml.

Schools

Sports Ground

STRATHMORE ROAD

STRATHMORE

Allotment Go

Nursery

Allotment Gardens, Div. & Muni Boro Bdy (U.D. Bdy)

TEDDINGTON CEMETERY

Mortuary Chapel (Ch. of England)

Mortuary Chapel (Nonconformist)

Stone

Stone

Stone

Stone

F.P. Stone Park,

S.P.

S.B.

S.P.

S.P.

Engine Shed

SOUTHFIE

F.P.

34. In 1935, a new booking office was built on the up side, close to the footbridge steps (right). The old building and running rail kerb are also evident. C.O.D. refers to a "cash on delivery" service then offered for parcels up to £40 in value. (N.Langridge coll.)

35. Photographed in 1971, the signal box lost its signals and junction function on 10th November 1974, when Feltham Panel took control of the area. It was used as a gate box until 25th March 1975, after which date the 1973 full lifting barriers were controlled from Feltham under CCTV. (D.Cullum)

36. New canopies were provided during the 1935 modernisation and are seen as unit no. 5846 arrives as the 15.15 Waterloo to Kingston service on 30th March 1989. The station was named after "Strawberry Hill", the 1776 Gothic style house associated with Horace Walpole and more recently used as a college. (J.Scrace)

BRITISH RAILWAYS (S)
This ticket is issued subject to the Bye-laws, Regulations and Conditions contained in the Publications and Notices of and applicable to the Railway Executive.
Available on DAY of issue ONLY.
Kingston to
LONDON
THIRD CLASS
Issued in exchange for L. T. (Green Line) Return Ticket issued by the London Transport Executive
NOT TRANSFERABLE.

0947   0947

37. Photographed on the same day, Strawberry Hill was unusual amongst suburban stations in that it retained most of its pre-war features, notably its fully enclosed footbridge. The lighting was updated again in October 1989. (J.Scrace)

2. SHEPPERTON BRANCH

FULWELL JUNCTION

38. Looking east from Stanley Road bridge in 1952, we see the fog signalman's hut (foreground), the junction signals (plus Strawberry Hill's distant), the former locomotive water tank and the EMU shed.   The box closed on 10th November 1974. (D.Cullum)

FULWELL

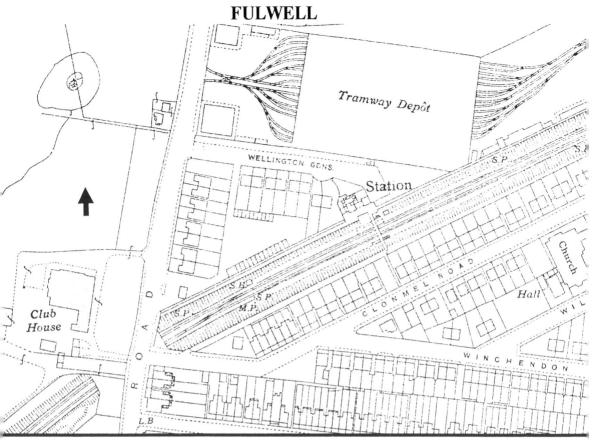

The 1934 edition shows that the station was well situated for the golf course and the high-density housing. The "Tramway Depot" had housed trolleybuses since 1931 but some of the tram rails remained visible 60 years after the conversion.

39. A westward view from Stanley Road bridge shows the station building on the right, remote from its platforms. Note the deep drainage channels each side of the track - necessary owing to water-bearing gravel through which the cutting passes. (Lens of Sutton)

40. A pre-electrification picture of indifferent quality is worth including as it shows the long forgotten signal box, which closed with the advent of electrification. Further west, Fulwell Cutting box was in use on race days until April 1969. In the background is the massive depot of London United Tramways, a serious competitor to the LSWR. (Lens of Sutton)

41. A 1962 view of the up platform reveals that only a waiting room was available at platform level. The house, booking office and toilets were at the end of Wellington Gardens, a road that was still unsurfaced in 1989. New nameboards in 1990 temporarily gave the station a Welsh appearance, as they were mispelt FULLWELL. (J.N.Faulkner)

SOUTHERN RAILWAY.
This ticket is issued subject to the Company's Bye-laws, Regulations & Conditions in their Time Tables, Notices and Book of Regulations.
Available on DAY of issue ONLY
KINGSTON to
Kingston   Kingston
Waterloo   Waterloo
WATERLOO
Third Class (38) Third Class
Fare 1/3   Fare 1/3
0008

42. A May 1989 photograph shows that the platforms have been totally rebuilt and retaining walls provided, work starting in January 1987. In the distance is the 62yd long tunnel, the scene of repeated flooding with consequent disruption to passenger services. Fulwell is not a parish - the name originates from a former farm nearby. (J.Scrace)

HAMPTON

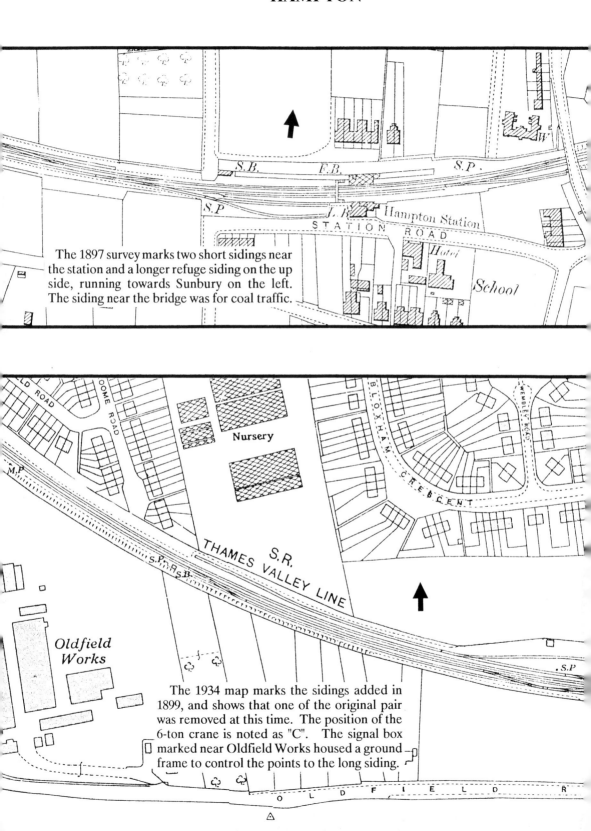

The 1897 survey marks two short sidings near the station and a longer refuge siding on the up side, running towards Sunbury on the left. The siding near the bridge was for coal traffic.

The 1934 map marks the sidings added in 1899, and shows that one of the original pair was removed at this time. The position of the 6-ton crane is noted as "C". The signal box marked near Oldfield Works housed a ground frame to control the points to the long siding.

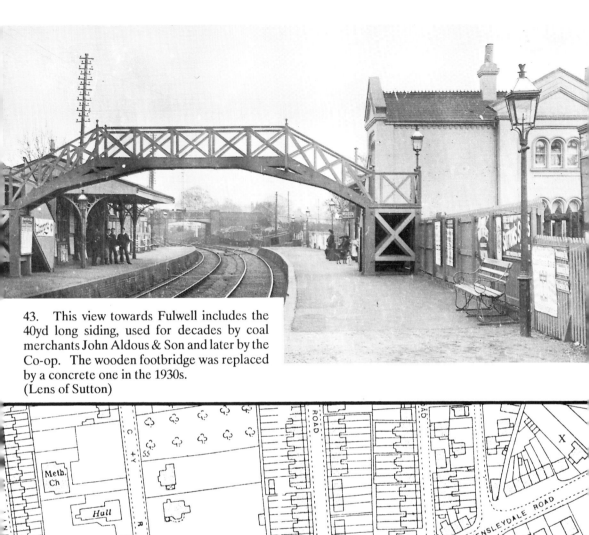

43. This view towards Fulwell includes the 40yd long siding, used for decades by coal merchants John Aldous & Son and later by the Co-op. The wooden footbridge was replaced by a concrete one in the 1930s.
(Lens of Sutton)

44. The train seen in picture 14 proceeded to the Shepperton branch and the rear coach is passing over the unusual level crossing. The gates visible were worked by hand when access was required to the small yard. Ferry vans of the type seen on the left were unloaded there at this time, having carried horsemeat from Hungary for a pet food manufacturer. (S.C.Nash)

Lower left

45. A gate wheel was provided in the signal box, which remained in use as a block post until 10th November 1973. Full barriers were fitted on 16th December 1973, these being controlled from Feltham under CCTV from 29th January 1975. The photograph was taken in January 1968. (J.Scrace)

46. After the closure of the goods yard on 3rd May 1965, the shed was sold and extended for commercial purposes. Cars are parked in the original small goods yard, which in the 1940s and 50s normally only received one loaded wagon per annum - 10 tons of coal for the station fireplaces. (J.M.Hooker)

47. The main entrance is seen in 1986. Early in 1989, the wooden walls of the booking hall were removed and the window on the left was enlarged to form a doorway into a new booking "hall". The building dates from about 1880, following the doubling of the line.
(V.Mitchell)

BRITISH RAILWAYS (S)
This ticket is issued subject to the Bye-laws, Regulations and Conditions contained in the Publications and Notices of and applicable to the Railway Executive.

Kingston to

Kingston
Teddington

Kingston
Teddington

TEDDINGTON

THIRD CLASS (S 40)   THIRD CLASS
Fare 4dH   Fare 4dH
NOT TRANSFERABLE.

48. An April 1989 photograph reveals that, unlike most suburban stations, Hampton's buildings had changed little. On the right is the palatial gentlemen's toilet, while in the centre there is the white-painted former stationmaster's office. His garden is now occupied by a large block of flats and shops which were built between the up platform and Ashley Road in 1990. (J.Scrace)

PERSONAL MEMORIES

Your author (VM) was born within sight of the branch (X marks the spot) and infant impressions of the local narrow gauge line led to an avid interest in such systems. This later contributed to an involvement in the founding of the Festiniog Railway Society and the line's revival.

Most non-school time was spent on the station, helping the staff and learning all aspects of railway operation. The station master would find routine clerical tasks, the booking clerk would allow selection and dating of tickets, the goods clerk found endless wagons to be swept out, the signalman always thought that his box needed further polishing and the senior porter seemed to have obsessions about platform sweeping and the polishing of brasswork.

All these tasks were a prelude to the granting of a very unofficial footplate pass for the shunting engine. This was invariably a class T9 4-4-0, no. 119 (the former royal engine) or no. 120 (now preserved) which arrived from Teddington (light engine) at about 8.50am. About 30 minutes earlier, a class 700 0-6-0 had struggled down the branch with the goods for all three stations. It dropped off some wagons for Hampton, for the T9 to shunt, and proceeded to Sunbury and Shepperton. Mid-morning, the T9 would transfer from the down yard to the up and shunt Aldous's siding. This involved hauling the train into the up platform, in order to run round it, and at the same time propelling Aldous's wagons. This was the opportunity to commence the illicit and greatly anticipated footplate ride. The T9 departed, light engine, at labout 12.50pm, its movement being a legacy of a school train which operated until 1939. There had been a similar afternoon trip for the benefit of pupils of Hampton Grammar School, which was situated close to the station until that time. The 700 returned, heavily laden, at about 1.20pm.

Of all the laborious tasks performed, the brasswork in the building featured in picture 48 was the most time consuming, this resulting in a lifelong interest in sanitary engineering.

Relief from the routine operation of the branch came when Fulwell Cutting flooded and steam trains were substituted between Hampton and Teddington. The usual procedure was to summon the M7 or T1 0-4-4T that spent much of the day shunting at Kingston. It collected a couple of coaches from the holiday trains that were berthed east of Teddington and waded through the water in Fulwell Tunnel to operate from the down platform at Hampton. The up side was used for an electric shuttle service to Shepperton.

On one occasion, after a severe thunderstorm, two elderly Maunsell coaches were waiting for the early morning crowds. Taking a corner seat, your author observed a solitary lavatory brush on the opposite seat. As the compartment filled, each seated individual denied ownership of the object until the final person placed it on the luggage rack, amidst the umbrellas and much sniggering. The crowd disembarked at Teddington and were jostled by a low ranking railwayman, demanding to know who was in possession of his brush. Apparently he had been instructed to clean eight coaches but two had suddenly disappeared, along with his valuable equipment, for which he, no doubt, had dutifully signed.

HAMPTON WATERWORKS

The Grand Junction Water Works Co. established works at Chelsea in 1820 and Kew Bridge in 1835, and supplied an area from Mayfair westwards. The Southwark & Vauxhall Water Co. was formed in 1845 and had a works at Battersea, which supplied South London as far as Nunhead.. In 1852, the Metropolis Water Act prohibited the abstraction of Thames water below Teddington Lock, which resulted in these companies building new works at Hampton. In 1902 they came under the control of the Metropolitan Water

Board whose programme of improvements included the provision of a 2ft gauge railway between the works at Kempton Park and Hampton, with a line to their coal bunkers at the wharf on the Thames. The line was opened in 1915 and three identical 0-4-2Ts were built by Kerr, Stuart & Co. (nos. 2366-2368) to work the line. A new works, with steam turbines and coal conveyors, was opened in 1936 and the railway closed within a few years.

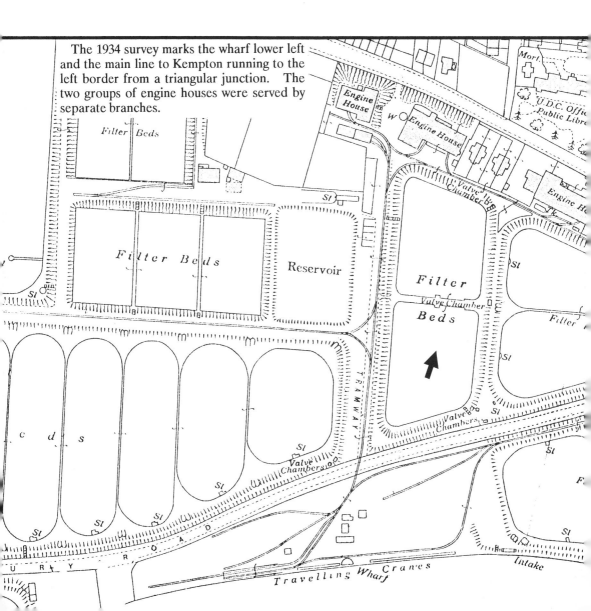

The 1934 survey marks the wharf lower left and the main line to Kempton running to the left border from a triangular junction. The two groups of engine houses were served by separate branches.

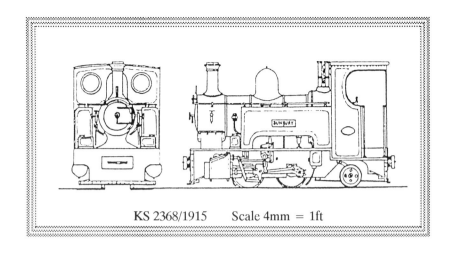

KS 2368/1915   Scale 4mm = 1ft

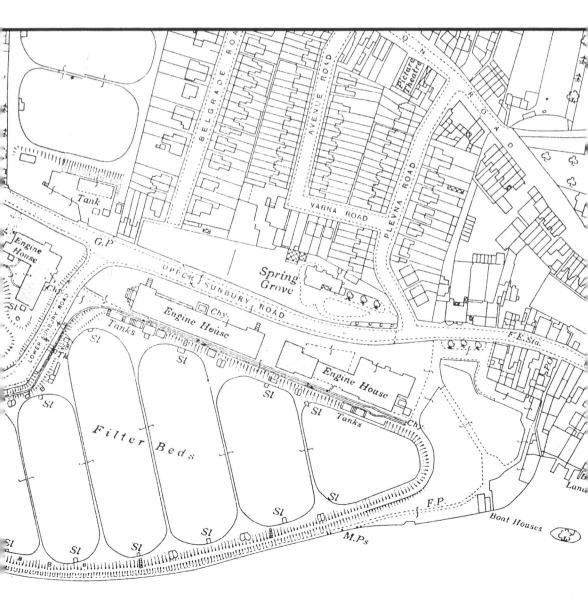

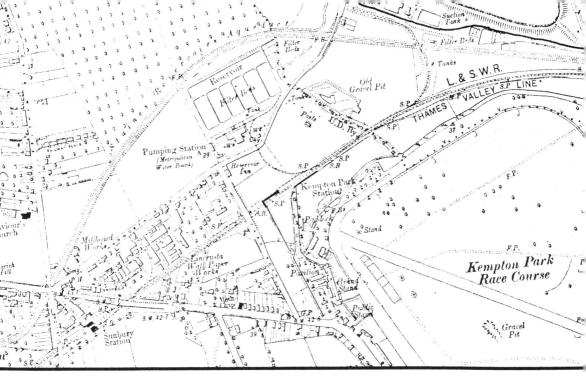

49. The engine houses contained massive beam engines which collectively consumed about 110 tons of coal daily. This arrived mainly by barge and was transferred by a high-level travelling crane into a large hopper, the end of which is seen on the left. It was then conveyed by rail to the pumping houses, first crossing over the Lower Sunbury Road by the trees. In times of flood or lighterman's strike, coal could be loaded from the LSWR at Kempton Park. (R.Shepherd coll.)

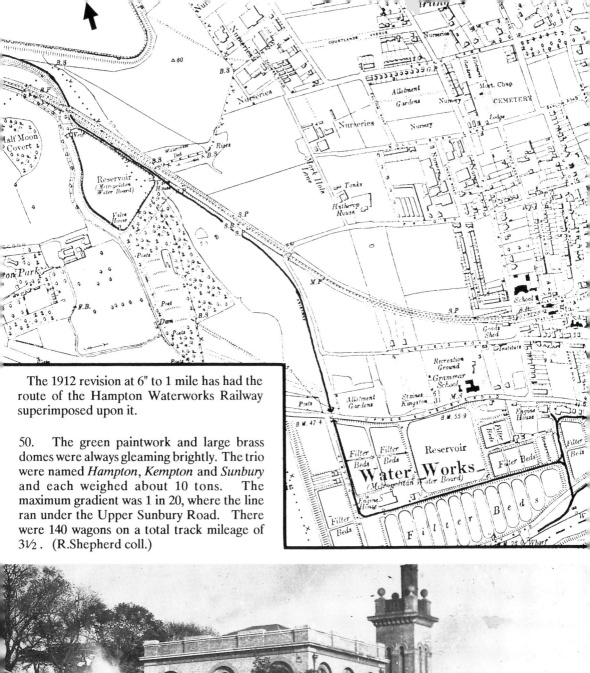

The 1912 revision at 6" to 1 mile has had the route of the Hampton Waterworks Railway superimposed upon it.

50. The green paintwork and large brass domes were always gleaming brightly. The trio were named *Hampton*, *Kempton* and *Sunbury* and each weighed about 10 tons. The maximum gradient was 1 in 20, where the line ran under the Upper Sunbury Road. There were 140 wagons on a total track mileage of 3½. (R.Shepherd coll.)

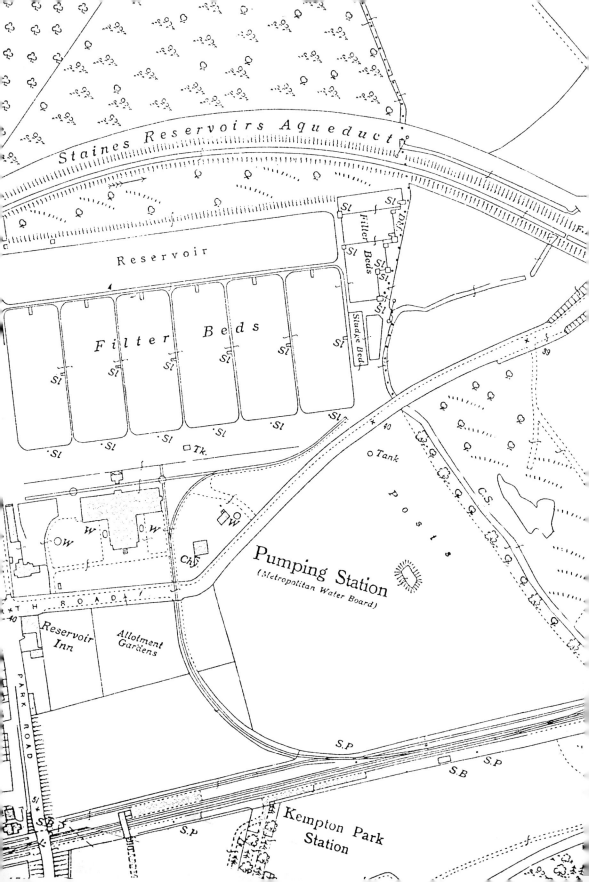

Staines Reservoirs Aqueduct

Reservoir

Filter Beds

Filter Beds

Sl

Sl

Sl

Sl

Sl

Sl

F i l t e r   B e d s

Sl

Sl

Sl

Sl

Sl

Sl

Sl

Sl

Sl

Sl

Sl

Sl

Sl

□ *Tk.*

Sludge Beds

39

40

o *Tank*

P o s t s

C S

W

W

Ch.

W

○ W

Pumping Station
(Metropolitan Water Board)

T H   R O A D

40

Reservoir
Inn

Allotment
Gardens

PARK ROAD

S.P

S.P

S.B

S.P

51

S.B

S.P

**Kempton Park
Station**

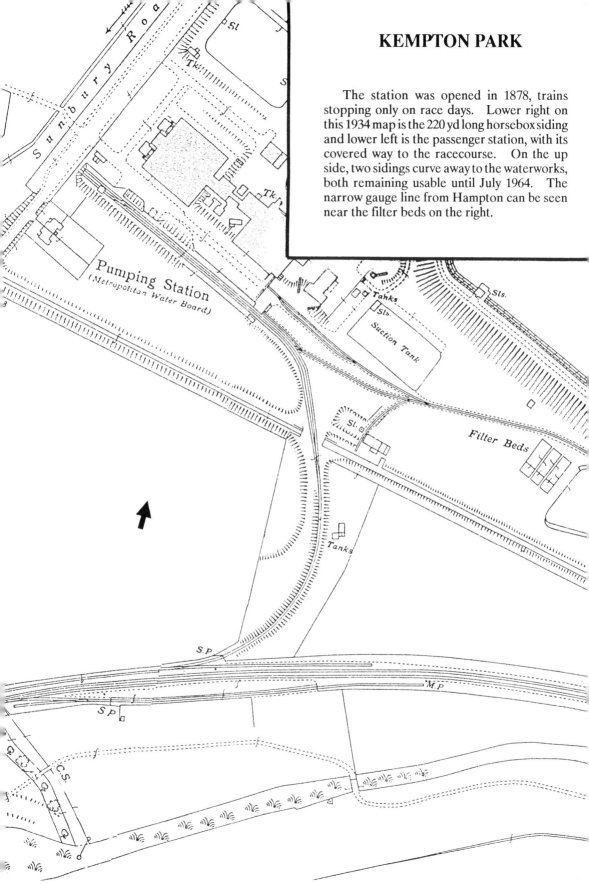

KEMPTON PARK

The station was opened in 1878, trains stopping only on race days. Lower right on this 1934 map is the 220 yd long horsebox siding and lower left is the passenger station, with its covered way to the racecourse. On the up side, two sidings curve away to the waterworks, both remaining usable until July 1964. The narrow gauge line from Hampton can be seen near the filter beds on the right.

Pumping Station
(Metropolitan Water Board)

Tanks

Sts

Sts

Suction Tank

St.

Filter Beds

Tanks

S.P.

M.P

S.P.

C.S.

51. Prisoners-of-war in their thousands arrived at Kempton Park for decontamination and interrogation in the latter part of WWII. Most trains were hauled by SR 4-6-0s or Austerity 2-8-0s, but LMS 4-4-0s and 4COR electrics were also noted. Corridor stock was always used, as fewer military guards were required to prevent escape. Note the non-electrified bay platform. (Lens of Sutton)

52. The bay platform (left) had been devoid of track for 16 years when photographed in 1980. Until October 1964, the numerous extra race trains necessitated the opening of two signal boxes between here and Hampton - Hanworth and Mark Hole. In 1937, 75,228 racegoers arrived here by rail - second only to Epsom. (T.Wright)

53. A class 455 unit rattles through the deserted platforms on 8th April 1989, bound for Shepperton. Prior to WWII, the intensive electric service was augmented by steam hauled trains for 1st class passengers, complicating the train movements at the end of the branch. Class M7 0-4-4Ts were normally used. (J.Scrace)

SUNBURY

54.   A westward view shows that the main buildings were on the down side, as was the signal box which remained in use until 9th March 1969.   77B is the LSWR set number, not a headcode.   (Lens of Sutton)

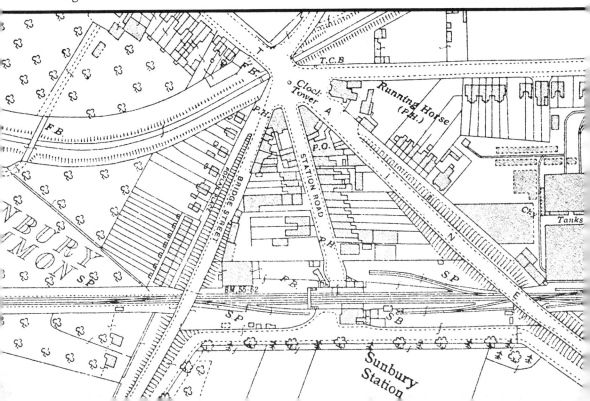

55. Looking east from Bridge Street bridge, we see the gated siding for Fear Bros. The public sidings were seen in the previous picture. In the background is the board factory, which also had private sidings. (Lens of Sutton)

Between Sunbury station (left centre) and Kempton Park (right border) were two non-electrified loops, each over 300 yds long. The private siding for Collis could accommodate twelve wagons and is shown curving north on this 1934 map.

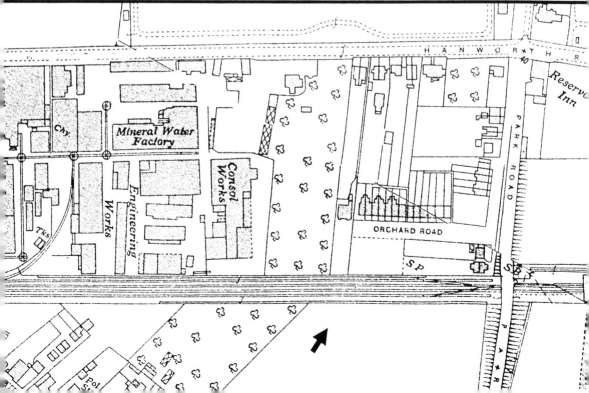

56. On race days and during most of WWII, the down line to Shepperton was used as a single line. The up line could then be used for the storage of empty stock, mainly defective wagons during the war. 4SUB no. 4530 crosses to the up line while working the 3.0pm from Shepperton on Easter Monday 1954. Note that permanent signalling was provided. (J.N.Faulkner)

57. The up side buildings were destroyed by a bomb on 29th November 1940 and were replaced by a temporary wooden structure. In 1965, Sunbury was provided with the dreary CLASP buildings, being one of the first to be so subjected. The concrete footbridge had arrived before WWII and is seen in 1989. (J.Scrace)

58. The rebuilt station is evident as unit no. 5726 leaves as the 12.41 Shepperton to Waterloo on 8th April 1989. The large sub-station in the background was redundant and had found commercial use by then. It had once housed rotary converters. (J.Scrace)

UPPER HALLIFORD

59. A halt was opened on 1st May 1944 for war-workers at the nearby factory of the British Thermostat Co. Owing to single line working, only a down platform was required. The second platform was opened on 6th May 1946, at about which time the company hired two 4COR sets for a works outing from the halt. Up to sixteen 8-coach trains would stand on the up line during Kempton Park race meetings, leaving gaps for occupation crossings only. This is the scene on 19th April 1954. (J.N.Faulkner)

O 169
SOUTHERN RAILWAY.
KEMPTON P'K·RACES
Available as advertised.
Sunbury to
MITCHAM
Via Wimbledon
Third Class Charge 4/1
FOR CONDITIONS
SEE BACK
SOUTHERN RAILWAY.
KEMPTON P'K·RACES
Available as advertised.
Mitcham to
SUNBURY
Via Wimbledon
& Admission to Kempton
Park Racecourse incl.
Entertainments-Duty.
Third Class Charge 4/1
O 169

61. The austere times in which it was built resulted in an all time low for railway architecture. Further west, a trailing siding from the down line served Lavender's premises from 1931 until 1938. (J.Scrace)

60. The rural peace had changed dramatically by the time the 11.16 from Waterloo was photographed on 8th April 1989. The M3 motorway runs on the north side of the railway at this point and the A244 passes over both. (J.Scrace)

SHEPPERTON

62. Class M7 no. 253 waits at the down platform prior to uncoupling and using the crossover. The up platform was a "white elephant" but would have been useful if the line had reached Chertsey as planned.
(Lens of Sutton)

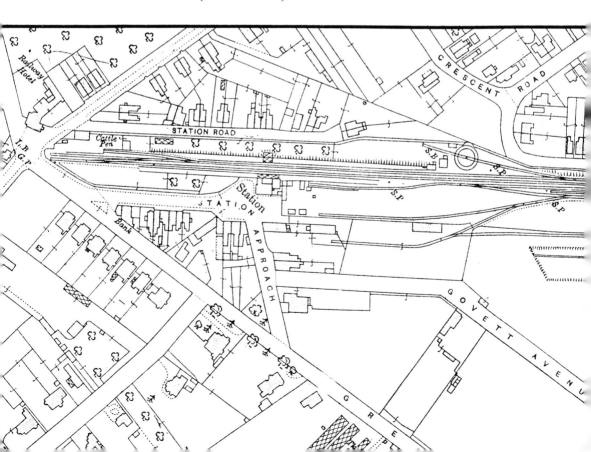

63. 4SUB no. 4201 waits to depart from the down platform, while another is stabled at the up platform on 8th November 1952. The architecture was similar to the three other original stations on the branch, although reverse slopes had been applied to the canopy by the SR. (D.Cullum)

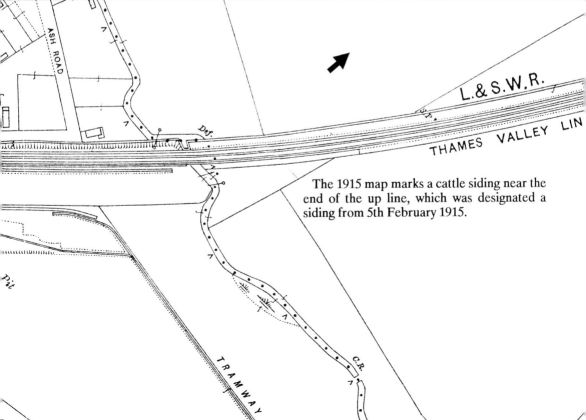

The 1915 map marks a cattle siding near the end of the up line, which was designated a siding from 5th February 1915.

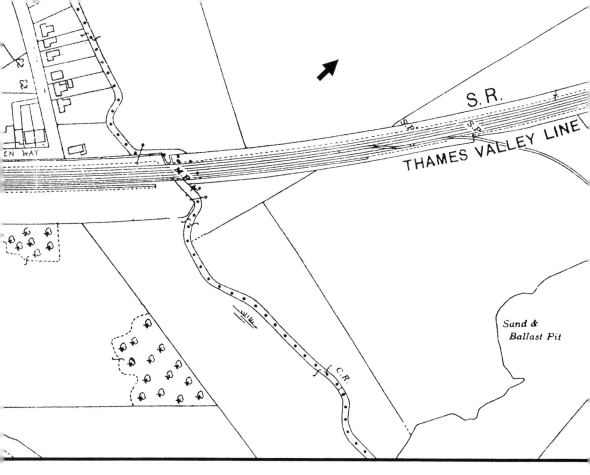

The 1934 survey includes a siding to a gravel pit (right) and the private siding for the Ferro Concrete Roof Plate Co. The turntable was removed in August 1942.

⟵

64. Waiting to return to Waterloo is 4SUB no. 4624. In the late 1950s, the signal arm for the down line was probably removed during the winter when single line working was unlikely. (D.Cullum coll.)

⟵

65. Sadly mass trespass brought steam rail-tours over electrified lines to an end. The LCGB's "Surrey Wanderer Special" on 5th July 1964 reached the end of the branch behind class M7 no. 30053, which subsequently went to the USA and returned to the Swanage Railway in 1988. (T.Wright)

66. Seen in May 1970, the signal box remained in use until 10th November 1974. The berthing sidings were still usable in 1990 but the goods sidings ceased to be used on 1st August 1960. (R.E.Ruffell)

67. Viewed over the buffer stops on 23rd October 1985, Departmental Unit no. 053 is coupled to ex-414 class no. 6142 in the up siding. The footbridge links the offices of Ian Allan Ltd., publishers of transport books and magazines. (T.Wright)

68. The former Pullman car *Malaga* brightened the view from the down plaltform in 1989. It was built in 1921, as a kitchen car, and modernised in 1949 for use in the "Golden Arrow". It was sold in 1962 and has subsequently been used by the publishing firm for business meetings and hospitality. (J.Scrace)

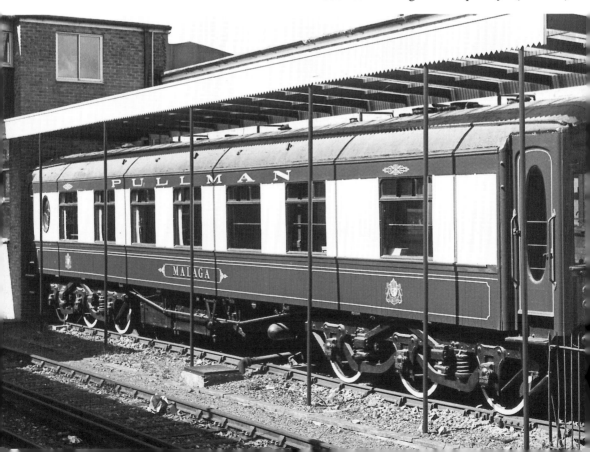

69. Unit no. 5733 is dwarfed by the new offices of Ian Allan Ltd on 8th April 1989. Terminal House and new station facilities were built as a joint project with BR, a far cry from the drab "CLASP" era. (J.Scrace)

70. A final look at the Shepperton branch includes no. 34100 *Appledore* leaving the terminus with a LCGB railtour on 4th February 1967, the last year of steam on the Southern Region. (S.C.Nash)

3. HOUNSLOW LOOP

BARNES

71. Opened with the line to Richmond on 27th July 1846, the station was, and still is, situated on Barnes Common. Quadrupling of the tracks westwards to Barnes was completed in 1886, this 1957 view showing the divergence of the lines to Richmond (left) and to Hounslow beyond the Junction Box. This box was subject to an arson attack by IRA terrorists in June 1921. (D.Cullum)

> **Other photographs of this station can be found in the *Waterloo to Windsor* album.**

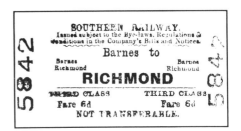

72. Semaphore signalling ceased on 22nd January 1959 when Barnes Power Box (right distance) came into use. Since 1976 it had controlled full barriers on the adjacent level crossing over Vine Road. The 9.55 Waterloo to Woking departs for Hounslow on 15th April 1989. (J.Scrace)

BARNES BRIDGE

73.   Opened on 12th March 1916, the high level platforms served a dense residential area, remote from tramways and other stations. Peak traffic was on the annual boat race day. (Lens of Sutton)

74.   The entrance to the booking hall was from The Terrace, the riverfront road. The passage on the right gave access to a public footpath across the river, on the downstream side of the railway. The passage now forms the entrance to the up platform as well and the shops have been converted to dwellings. (Lens of Sutton)

75. The partially tiled booking hall and the subway from it were closed in 1990, when ticket machines were installed on the platforms. The poster refers to the event described in captions 5 and 6. (Lens of Sutton)

```
2nd · SINGLE      SINGLE · 2nd
         Barnes Bridge   to
N  Barnes Bridge            Barnes Bridge  N
O  Barnes                        Barnes    O
        BARNES
4                                          4
00  (S)    3d. FARE  3d.    (S)   00
    For condit'ns see over  For condit'ns see over
```

77. A June 1988 photograph shows the irregular level of the up platform and the position of its buildings, which were demolished in 1990. At this time, new steps to both platforms were provided, both flights being devoid of roofing. (J.Scrace)

76. A train from Hounslow crosses the bow-string spans of Barnes Bridge on 24th January 1954, the public footpath being visible on the right. Single line working was in force for much of 1975-76, during major repair work on the bridge. Back in 1895, the bridge had been reconstructed but the original down span was retained (left) and the LSWR charged boat race spectators a high fee for use of this favoured position. (Pamlin Prints)

CHISWICK

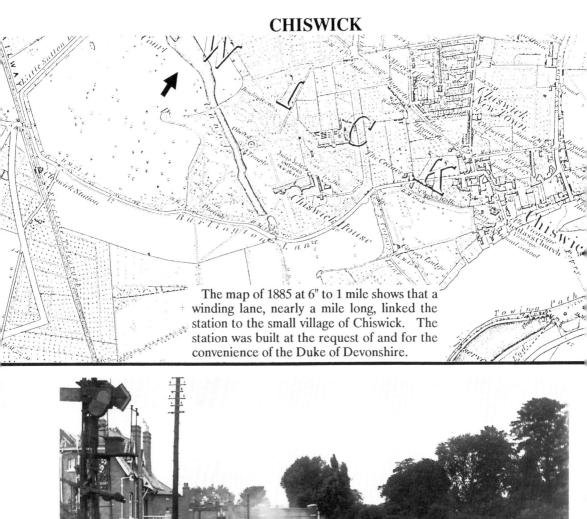

The map of 1885 at 6" to 1 mile shows that a winding lane, nearly a mile long, linked the station to the small village of Chiswick. The station was built at the request of and for the convenience of the Duke of Devonshire.

78. An up train from Hounslow passes under Sutton Lane and is seen from the station footbridge. On the right is the original single siding, which ceased to be used in March 1934. (Lens of Sutton)

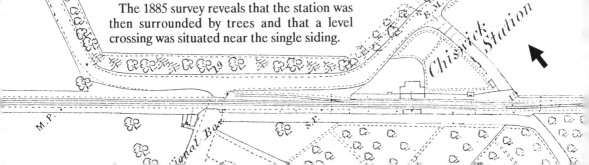

The 1885 survey reveals that the station was then surrounded by trees and that a level crossing was situated near the single siding.

79. The main buildings are on the up platform and were still standing in 1990. This view, from about 1960, shows the station to be still gaslit, nearly 50 years after electric traction was introduced. (Lens of Sutton)

80. The Great Chertsey Road (A316) was built in the 1930s and passes over the line in the distance. Little had changed by 1990, apart from the replacement of the down platform shelter by a glazed arch type and closure of the goods yard on 14th June 1958. (Lens of Sutton)

81. Unit no. 5870 forms the 15.25 Waterloo to Weybridge service on 14th June 1988, the year in which trains terminated alternately there and at Woking. The signal box had been closed on 19th March 1961, having replaced an earlier structure on 11th June 1944.
(J.Scrace)

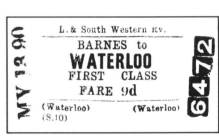

MY 13 90

L. & South Western Ry.

BARNES to
WATERLOO
FIRST CLASS
FARE 9d

(Waterloo)   (Waterloo)
(S.10)

6472

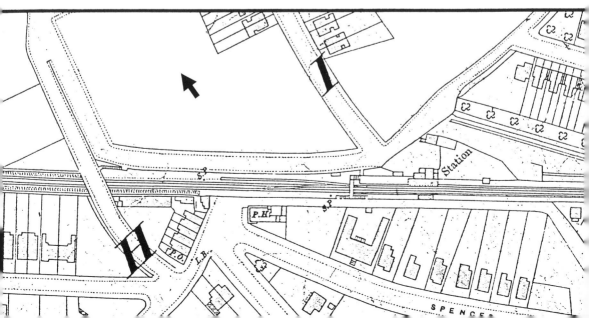

82. Grove Park crossing is about 500 yards west of Chiswick station and was fitted with barriers on 2nd September 1973. The house is remarkably close to the box, which was closed on 4th December 1974 when CCTV was installed. (J.Scrace)

SOUTHERN RAILWAY.
Issued subject to the Bye-laws, Regulations & Conditions in the Company's Bills and Notices.

Chiswick to

Chiswick
Wandsworth Town

Chiswick
Wandsworth Town

WANDSWORTH TOWN
Via Barnes Bridge

THIRD CLASS
Fare 6½d.

THIRD CLASS
Fare 6½d.

NOT TRANSFERABLE.

The 1912 edition shows housing development in progress and the consequent extension of sidings to accommodate the associated increase in coal traffic, in particular. Later, a crane of 4 tons 13 cwt capacity was provided.

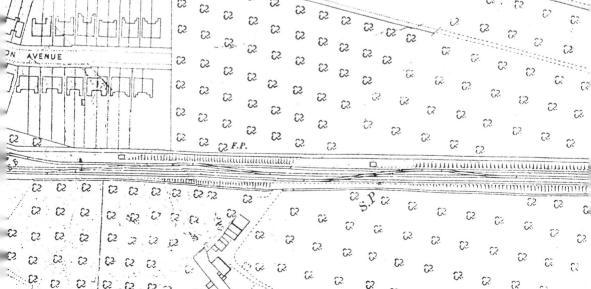

EAST OF KEW BRIDGE

83.   The up lines are duplicated for 220 yds east of New Kew Junction, the northern one being used for terminating trains from Willesden Junction until 12th September 1940, when that service was withdrawn.   No. 47177 is on the "Third Road" on 4th August 1977, with a Worksop to Eastbourne excursion.   The track was still used by inter-regional freight trains in 1990. (J.Scrace)

The 1st edition map of the area at 6" to 1 mile was compiled in 1871-83 and has the Hounslow Loop running across the sheet, Chiswick station being just beyond the right border. The LSWR line from Richmond is at the lower edge and passes through Brentford Road station (Gunnersbury since 1871) and curves to the right to Hammersmith. At the top is the North & South Western Junction line from Acton and Willesden Junction. On the left of its triangular junction an "Old Station" is marked. This was in use by passengers from August 1853 until October 1866, although N&SWJR trains ceased to call there regularly after 1st February 1862, when services were transferred to the station at the eastern corner of the triangle - "Kew Bridge". The "Chiswick Curve" was in use from 1st June 1870 until 9th May 1932, when the land was sold for the Chiswick Village scheme.

84.   New Kew Junction was opened on 1st February 1862 and was still described as such over a century later. The Brentford wholesale fruit market is in the background of this 1967 photograph of the box which closed on 28th July 1974. (J.Scrace)

The 1935 survey has the line from Hounslow on the left, from Willesden Junction at the top and from Barnes on the right. The LMS goods yard is within the triangle, the SR "Old Yard" being below it and "New Yard" to the left. The Old Yard was lifted in 1964 and the New Yard followed in 1977. On the left of the map are two running lines, two relief roads and a siding. All but the first pair were removed in 1977. The water works building is now occupied by the Kew Bridge Steam Museum and outside it there is a 2ft gauge railway on which operates ex-Penrhyn Railway 0-4-0ST *Lilla*.

Potomac
(Fish Pond)

LIONEL ROAD

D.Fn

Lodge

T.C.B.

G R E A T

W.M.

WAR MEMORIAL PARK

Lodge

Kew Bridge Goods Depôt

S.P.

S.P.

S.P.

S.P.

M.P.

Old Kew Junction   S.P.

S.B.

GREEN DRAGON LANE

30

School

Filter Beds

Filter Beds

Allotment Gardens

Filter Bed

Filter Beds

35

35

40

Reservoir

Reservoir

Kew Bridge Water W

(Met. Water Board)

Chapel Alley

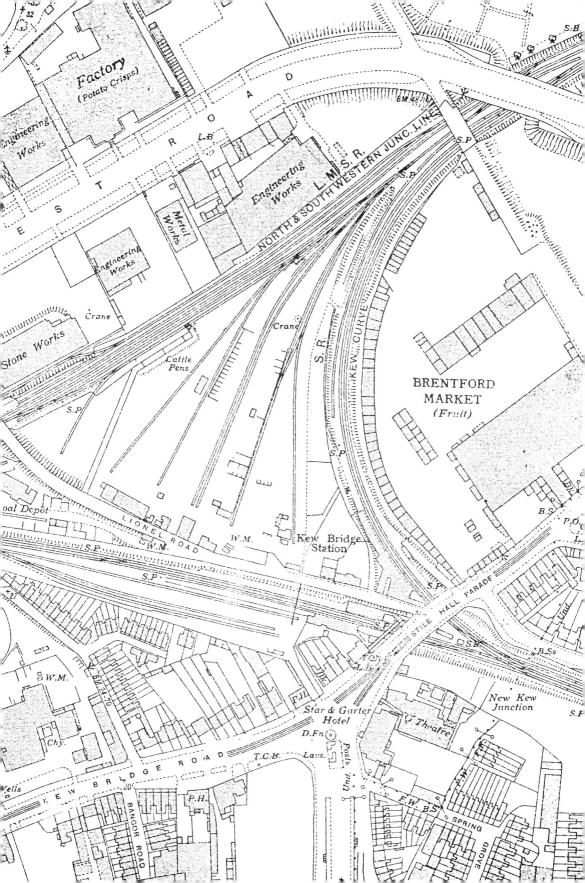

85. The former N&SWJR or LMS platforms are seen in about 1950, with New Kew Junction box beyond the bridge. The shunt signal is for the "Third Road" - after 1974 there was no opportunity to cross the up line here. (Lens of Sutton)

86. The former LMS arrival platform shelter had been converted to a store when photographed in 1956. Four rail electrification had been in use for passenger services until their cessation in 1940, the route having been a branch from the LMS Broad Street - Richmond line. (D.Cullum)

87. Ex-SECR class D no. 31577 heads north with "The Woburn Park Special", bringing a rare sight of a passenger train at the neglected platforms. (D.Cullum coll.)

88. Looking east from the former LSWR up platform in 1959, we see New Kew Junction and the three lines, beyond the bridge. The booking office on the N&SWJ platforms was closed on 1st July 1918 and the station demolished in 1920. Passengers then used an entrance beyond the building on the left. The subway under Lionel Road still remains. (D.Cullum coll.)

89. A westward view shows the differing styles of canopy and steam-hauled coaches berthed in the Old Yard. In 1948, BR designated this "South Yard" and the former LMS depot became "North Yard". (Lens of Sutton)

90. The exterior is seen in 1973 when it was no longer obscured by trolleybus wires. In 1990, the building was vacated and a new access to the footbridge provided, where the telephone box is located. (J.Scrace)

91. A 1988 picture reveals that the up platform canopy had been demolished - the down one followed two years later. The covered footbridge remained, but unglazed. Now unstaffed, the station simply possesses two ticket machines and two shelters, devoid of walls. (J.Scrace)

92. The first N&SWJR station is in the centre of this picture taken from Old Kew Junction box in July 1920. The building survived until 1956 but parts of the platform were still visible in 1968. The line on the left, to Willesden Junction, was subject to permissive working to Kew East Junction (LMS), i.e. goods trains could just queue up on it, not separated by signals. The coal yard on the right was the site of the first sidings in the district, as shown on the 6" scale map. (K.Nunn/LCGB)

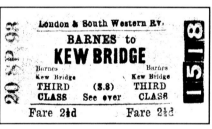

93. This box replaced one in the fork of the lines on 18th October 1942 and was in use until 8th September 1974. Behind it, in this 1968 photograph, are condemned BR containers standing in part of New Yard. The junction was greatly simplified in November 1981, with four points and no crossings. (J.Scrace)

BRENTFORD

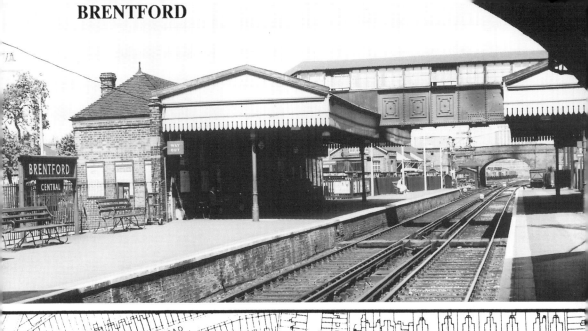

95. The signal box was on the east side of Windmill Road bridge and took over the function of Brentford Yard Box in May 1932. The suffix "Central" was added to the station name in 1950, although the GWR branch had ceased to carry passengers in 1942. The suffix was deleted on 12th May 1980.
(Lens of Sutton)

94. Brentford is a riverside town of great antiquity, noted for the Battles of Brentford in 1016 and 1642. The Grand Union Canal and a branch of the GWR both reached the Thames here. This view towards London includes the goods shed and Windmill Road bridge, beyond which is the six-siding goods yard. (Lens of Sutton)

96. No. 35028 *Clan Line* has been seen on many special trains in recent years and is here hauling a SCTS railtour on the up line on 5th June 1966. The goods yard had closed on 4th January 1965 but the crane (9tons 2 cwt) is still standing on the dock. Parcel traffic ceased on 7th September 1980. (J.Scrace)

97. The exterior was recorded in 1974 and in 1990 the main building was still standing, but the canopies and footbridge had gone. The quadruple track between Brentford and Old Kew Junction had been reduced to double in December 1966. (J.Scrace)

SYON LANE

98. The station was opened on 5th July 1931 and was provided with the standard SR steel canopy on the up side (left). Beyond Syon Lane bridge there was a trailing siding for Booth's Distillery until 1969. The line also passed under the GWR Brentford branch. (Lens of Sutton)

99. Seen in June 1988, all these structures were swept away in 1990 and replaced with two curved roofs on stilts. The station serves a large residential area and is convenient for Syon Park. In the early 1930s, many factories were built along the nearby newly-opened Great West Road. (J.Scrace)

100. No. 47526 *Northumbria* puts in a rare appearance with the 17.24 Old Oak Common to Ascot empty stock working on 15th June 1988. It would form the 18.43 Ascot to Manchester train for racegoers. (J.Scrace)

101. Wood Lane crossing is less than 500 yards from Isleworth and was fitted with barriers on 22nd July 1973, the box closing on 23rd December 1974 when CCTV was provided. No. E6024 approaches with an up freight on 25th July 1969. The first terminus was sited here and named "Hounslow" until more truthfully termed "Smallberry Green", four months after its opening on 22nd August 1849. (J.Scrace)

ISLEWORTH

102. The station opened on 1st February 1850, when Smallberry Green closed, and became Spring Grove & Isleworth in 1855, reverting to Isleworth in August 1911. This view features the wooden down platform, prior to 1911. (Lens of Sutton)

103. The main entrance was well situated on London Road and the station was conveniently close to a number of schools. This is another pre-1911 photograph. (Lens of Sutton)

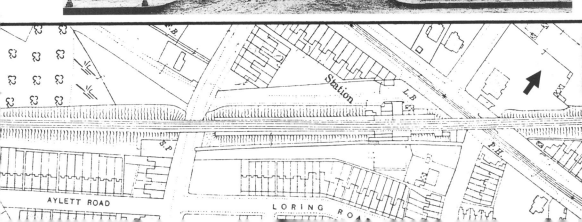

104. The negative was marked "3.44 Down", but the date was, unfortunately, not recorded. It was probably 19th century as the potentially dangerous practice of covering sleepers with ballast was outlawed before 1900. (Lens of Sutton)

105. Only the up side canopy had gone when the 14.25 Waterloo to Guildford service arrived on 20th June 1989, only the second month of operation to this destination. The 1990 modernisations had affected this station, by August. (J.Scrace)

← The 1915 edition shows that housing development was already complete and that there was a competitive street tramway. It was part of the Hounslow - Hammersmith route.

HOUNSLOW

106. The station, seen from the London end, was opened on 1st February 1850, when Isleworth ceased to be a terminus. In the early years, the rather cramped goods yard had a crossover between the far mineral wagon and the dock siding, beyond the goods shed. The site is now occupied by an industrial estate. (Lens of Sutton)

The 1934 survey shows the layout at its optimum, with two electrified berthing sidings west of the station.

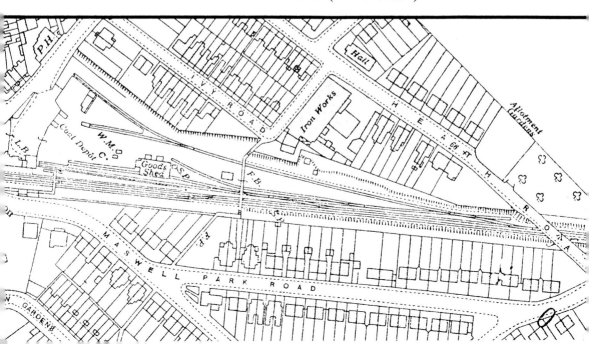

107. An unusual visitor was "Mr Drummond's Car". Built by and for the locomotive superintendent in 1898, it was known by fearful employees as "The Bug". It was fitted with table, chairs, buffet, lavatory and a port hole, through which orders could be given to the driver. Mr. Drummond's average annual mileage was 14,275. The headcode indicates that the photograph was taken after December 1917. (Lens of Sutton)

108.   No. 1 was one of two class H12 railcars built in 1904 for the Basingstoke & Alton line, where they were a dismal failure.   It subsequently worked the Bishops Waltham branch and was tried on the Burnham - Highbridge service, before being transferred to Strawberry Hill Depot to work the Twickenham - Gunnersbury route, via Hounslow, until 1914. (Lens of Sutton)

109.   One of the thirteen class H13 railcars broke down at Hounslow and was shunted into the down carriage sidings.   Class 0395 no. 404 was summoned from Strawberry Hill but it too failed and class G6 no. 267 had to come to their rescue, bearing the special train disc on the buffer beam.   How lucky we are that there was a camera to hand.   (Lens of Sutton)

110. The GNR loaned seven of their class J4 0-6-0s to the LSWR between 1917 and 1920. No. 646 waits with a down freight while LSWR no. 633 stands in the goods yard. The headcode is Brentford to Twickenham, via Whitton Junction. Further east, Hounslow No. 2 Coal Yard, composed of three long sidings on the up side, was in use from 1932 until 1973. (Lens of Sutton)

111. Another photograph from the LSWR era, reveals the details of the fully glazed footbridge (one still survives at Alton) and also includes the public footbridge. The 3SUB is no. E24. Many of these wooden-bodied vehicles, with their alphabetic headcodes, remained in use until 1961. (D.Cullum coll.)

112. A 3SUB emerges from Whitton Road bridge, passing a classical LSWR lower quadrant co-acting arm, and the up berthing siding, on the left. Photographed from out- side the signal box, unit no. 1232 was lengthened in October 1935 to become stand- ard with the Eastern and Central Section units. (Lens of Sutton)

113. The up berthing siding is seen from the down platlform in about 1960. Note that the starting signal had been given better visibility by moving it to the east side of the bridge. (Lens of Sutton)

114. In August 1974, the ground frame near Heath Road bridge was moved from its hut and a new one positioned further west, as all but one siding (to the Bay) were removed at that time. Goods traffic had ceased on 1st May 1968. (J.Scrace)

115. The West Thurrock to Micheldever oil train was photographed from the cat walk of the down berthing siding on 28th August 1974. The locomotive is no. 37261. (J.Scrace)

116. The signal box, visible in the background of the previous picture, closed on 7th September 1974. Behind it is the down electrified siding, which was taken out of use on 30th June 1974, the up one following later. (J.Scrace)

117.   Two photographs from March 1989, complete our survey of Hounslow.   Apart from the modern signs, cars, and telephone, the picture would be undatable. Subsequently a new booking office was fitted out in the single storey wing on the left and most of the remainder of the building let out to a builders merchant. (J.Scrace)

118.   The wooden footbridge, seen in earlier photographs, had long been replaced by the standard SR concrete type.   The down side buildings (right) were replaced by a simple glass roofed shelter in 1990.   (J.Scrace)

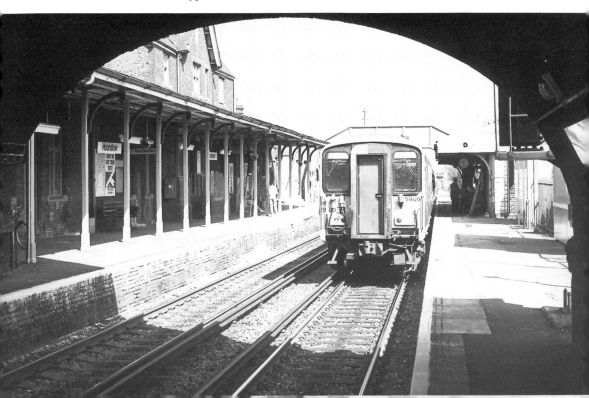

HOUNSLOW JUNCTION

119. The box is situated at the northern apex of the triangular junction with the Twickenham-Feltham line, remaining in use until 8th September 1974. The other two boxes can be seen in pictures 79 and 80 in our *Waterloo to Windsor* album. (J.Scrace)

120. No. 73005 proceeds from the Feltham direction with the 09.48 Earley to Hoo Junction service on 28th August 1974. The curve to the left to Whitton Junction was opened on 1st January 1883 and was only used by a few peak hour trains after May 1987. Trains via Hounslow have subsequently given a greatly improved service to stations as far south as Guildford. (J.Scrace)

MP Middleton Press

Easebourne Lane, Midhurst. West Sussex. GU29 9AZ
(0730) 813169

Write or telephone for our latest booklist

BRANCH LINES

BRANCH LINES TO MIDHURST
BRANCH LINES AROUND MIDHURST
BRANCH LINES TO HORSHAM
BRANCH LINES TO EAST GRINSTEAD
BRANCH LINES TO ALTON
BRANCH LINE TO HAYLING
BRANCH LINE TO TENTERDEN
BRANCH LINES TO NEWPORT
BRANCH LINES TO TUNBRIDGE WELLS
BRANCH LINE TO SWANAGE
BRANCH LINES TO LONGMOOR
BRANCH LINE TO LYME REGIS
BRANCH LINE TO FAIRFORD
BRANCH LINE TO ALLHALLOWS
BRANCH LINES AROUND ASCOT
BRANCH LINES AROUND WEYMOUTH
BRANCH LINE TO HAWKHURST
BRANCH LINES AROUND EFFINGHAM JN
BRANCH LINE TO MINEHEAD

SOUTH COAST RAILWAYS

CHICHESTER TO PORTSMOUTH
BRIGHTON TO EASTBOURNE
RYDE TO VENTNOR
EASTBOURNE TO HASTINGS
PORTSMOUTH TO SOUTHAMPTON
HASTINGS TO ASHFORD
SOUTHAMPTON TO BOURNEMOUTH
ASHFORD TO DOVER
BOURNEMOUTH TO WEYMOUTH
DOVER TO RAMSGATE

SOUTHERN MAIN LINES

HAYWARDS HEATH TO SEAFORD
EPSOM TO HORSHAM
CRAWLEY TO LITTLEHAMPTON
THREE BRIDGES TO BRIGHTON
WATERLOO TO WOKING
VICTORIA TO EAST CROYDON
TONBRIDGE TO HASTINGS
EAST CROYDON TO THREE BRIDGES
WOKING TO SOUTHAMPTON
WATERLOO TO WINDSOR
LONDON BRIDGE TO EAST CROYDON

COUNTRY RAILWAY ROUTES

BOURNEMOUTH TO EVERCREECH JN
READING TO GUILDFORD
WOKING TO ALTON
BATH TO EVERCREECH JUNCTION
GUILDFORD TO REDHILL
EAST KENT LIGHT RAILWAY
FAREHAM TO SALISBURY
BURNHAM TO EVERCREECH JUNCTION
REDHILL TO ASHFORD
YEOVIL TO DORCHESTER
ANDOVER TO SOUTHAMPTON

LONDON SUBURBAN RAILWAYS

CHARING CROSS TO DARTFORD
HOLBORN VIADUCT TO LEWISHAM
KINGSTON & HOUNSLOW LOOPS

STEAMING THROUGH

STEAMING THROUGH EAST HANTS
STEAMING THROUGH SURREY
STEAMING THROUGH WEST SUSSEX
STEAMING THROUGH THE ISLE OF WIGHT
STEAMING THROUGH WEST HANTS

OTHER RAILWAY BOOKS

GARRAWAY FATHER & SON
LONDON CHATHAM & DOVER RAILWAY
INDUSTRIAL RAILWAYS OF THE S. EAST
WEST SUSSEX RAILWAYS IN THE 1980s
SOUTH EASTERN RAILWAY - due late 1990

OTHER BOOKS

MIDHURST TOWN THEN & NOW
EAST GRINSTEAD THEN & NOW

WALKS IN THE WESTERN HIGH WEALD
TILLINGBOURNE BUS STORY

MILITARY DEFENCE OF WEST SUSSEX
BATTLE OVER SUSSEX 1940

SURREY WATERWAYS
KENT AND EAST SUSSEX WATERWAYS
HAMPSHIRE WATERWAYS